Riding Waves

New Women's Voices Series, No. 137

poems by

Kathryn Jordan

Finishing Line Press
Georgetown, Kentucky

Riding Waves

New Women's Voices Series, No. 137

Copyright © 2018 by Kathryn Jordan
ISBN 978-1-63534-422-6 First Edition
All rights reserved under International and Pan-American Copyright Conventions. No part of this book may be reproduced in any manner whatsoever without written permission from the publisher, except in the case of brief quotations embodied in critical articles and reviews.

ACKNOWLEDGMENTS

"Tape" is the 2016 winner of San Miguel de Allende Writers' Conference Prize for Poetry

Thanks to Alison Luterman, my wonderful mentor, and Eliot Jordan, my husband and first reader.

Publisher: Leah Maines
Editor: Christen Kincaid
Cover Art: Kathryn Jordan
Author Photo: Ben Krantz
Cover Design: Elizabeth Maines McCleavy

Printed in the USA on acid-free paper.
Order online: www.finishinglinepress.com
          also available on amazon.com

                Author inquiries and mail orders:
                      Finishing Line Press
                          P. O. Box 1626
                    Georgetown, Kentucky 40324
                              U. S. A.

Table of Contents

Tustin Arms, 1966 1

The Fall 2

Darkness 3

Books and Matches 4

Little Miss Sunbeam 5

My Brother's Eyes 6

The Dead and the Living 7

Song of Orpheus 8

Tiny Bubbles 9

Diapause 10

The Watch Commander 11

Death Portrait 12

Youth with White Deck Shoes 13

Where the Power Lies 14

Attitude 15

Green Heron, Hunting 17

Coming to My Senses 18

Ghost Breast 19

Moon on the North Platte 20

What's Lost 21

Riding Waves 23

Yearly Rituals 24

Tape 25

Vanishing Point 28

To my mother's sensuality and my father's fighting spirit; to Eliot, Aurelia, and James Jordan for teaching me to ride the waves with conviction and love.

Tustin Arms, 1966

The window, adorned by a prickly cactus,
yields a small horizon: stubble
of newly built townhouses, pimpled here
and there by giant piles of burning orange trees,
smoldering in black heat. My mom says
my dad is dropping something called
Napalm on the forests of Vietnam.

I want to run through orchards again, sweet
scent of citrus blossom, but it's either hide
from boys hurling baseball-hard oranges
or sneak with them
to lie down in tall clover.
For now, I'll ride on the back
of that sting ray with the kid
who never asks my name.

It's late and I creep down shag carpet,
following sound threads, find
my mother entangled on her bed
with an old friend from back home.
How could you?
I shout, ram my poster-covered door
in its jamb, slam the lock. She pounds
the wood with the palm
of her hand, insists
everything's alright.
Come out, please.

The Fall

My mother said, *Isn't this great? We get to
live right next door to Disneyland!* And it was
great: active military got free passes to go
scream on the Matterhorn and bob in a little boat,
admiring hundreds of wooden babushkas opening
and closing their painted mouths, "It's a Small
World," peace and love pouring out.

We moved 3,000 miles to Tustin to be closer
to Dad in Vietnam. I watched my mother
arrange furniture in our little apartment, endure
TV news reports of pilots shot down over fields
of fire. Sometimes we listened to the tapes
Dad sent from Vietnam, watched the black
recorder nod, prisoner of spindle and gear.

She tried to keep up, cut blue crepe paper
to make a skirt, dyed mop head orange
for me to be Raggedy Anne for Halloween.
I watched her get ready to go out after working
all day at Bullock's jewelry counter. She put
TV dinners in the oven, sat at her vanity,
pinned a fake blonde pony tail to her head.
It's called a fall, she said, as she sprayed My Sin
in a tinted crystal atomizer on her neck.

My little brother and I peered through
the Venetian blinds as she backed out
of the carport, then turned on our perfect
family on TV: "My Three Sons" with
Fred McMurray and his chuckling pipe.
I'm just glad no one told me Fred was a killer
in "Double Indemnity." I needed him more
than he ever knew.

Darkness

Some days I get off the school bus and there she is,
I can see her from way down the street, swaggering
in that sparkly outfit, hips rolling side to side as she
paces in our yard. I know she's been drinking
and I set my face to meet her loneliness
and hide my own. But, sometimes

> my back feels her hand, guiding me around the room,
> *Your father is a wonderful dancer,* she says as she dips me.
> I grow wings when we dance, and when we polka,
> knees high, she flies like when she was my angel.

She's out tonight with those nineteen-year-old girls—the ones
who showed me the Watusi. I had to stay home because I'm only
twelve. Besides, I have to take care of my little brother sleeping
in the next room. Now I'm awake because of a noise. The red
dial on my clock says 4:00 and it's dark in the house.
My heart pounds, I'm listening so hard.

I'll fight, I'll throw rubbing alcohol in his face, whoever he is.
After I pour some into a bottle cap, the phone rings and it's my stepdad,
calling from Yuma—*She's asleep,* I lie—saying he'll be home tomorrow
from the hop with his squadron. Such a silly word for bombing in the
desert.

Tomorrow, she'll come home, bring cinnamon rolls with pecans.
I'll eat too much and forget all about it.

Books and Matches

That summer my mother took up residence
as Queen of the Lariat Bar, leaving fourteen-
year-old me tumbling loose in the Rockies,
I told those cowboys I was sixteen because
I wanted to lead horseback rides. No one knew
I'd learned to ride from books. The first time
I sat a saddle, leather smells like her wallet, I held
my back erect, squeezed my thighs around the haunch,
and let the reins tell me of the horse's mouth.

Plodding geldings and mares, dusty, heavy
with tourists from the city, picking our way up
the mountain, me at the head of the line
on a dapple gray, lighting a Salem, holding
the match book pinched between two fingers
my cupped hand forming a wind-block, using
my thumb to strike flame.
This I had learned from boys,
not books.

Little Miss Sunbeam

Whenever a tourist said, *Give me a spirited horse!!* you could
count the minutes on one hand and here'd come the horse
trotting back to the barn, red-faced rider yanking on the reins,
sputtering, *This horse is no damned good!* The only thing for it
was to mount up and lead the would-be riders to the mountain.

In the afternoons, the cowboys' girlfriends drove up, long blonde hair,
surly beauties in denim. Debbie Peterson and Jan Dickinson leaned
against their cars, lazily asking where we could go drink a case
of Coors, calling each other "Peter" and "Dick" in a way I thought
risqué. But, they rescued me from popping corn at the snack bar,
got me work waitressing: pouring coffee, taking orders, slathering
oil from a tin on *Little Miss Sunbeam* toast as the owl-eyed owner
watched us in white chef's cap, carving roast beef in the window.

Six mornings a week at five-thirty, Debbie honked her horn,
Chevy Impala rumbling down at the road's end. Out of the cottage,
I scampered, blithe as the mist rising from the green lake, dawn
not yet crept around Mt.Baldy, not a ripple to be seen. After work,
and after I'd hung around up at the stables, I sat with Jan in her room,
listening to the Who: *See me, feel me, touch me, heal me.*

I was a hanger-on, a pretender, but they all accepted me—
the cowboys, the girls, Danny, the older boy they introduced
me to, with his sloppy kisses, all of us fishtailing around
switchbacks on Trail Ridge Road, windows down, boys
slouching behind steering wheels, girls laughing, knees
drawn up against dashboards, *In the Summertime* on the dial.

I was fourteen and I laughed loudly, driving that spirited
horse out again and again, away from the barn
and from who I'd been.

My Brother's Eyes

My fifteenth summer, my mother left us at sunset
to go to town and my brother tumbled downstairs night after
night, eyes wide, trembling. Folding in what I know now:
he was ripe for picking by the man at Mountain Mini-Golf,
who offered free games, found our mother on her stool
at the Lariat Bar, bought beer, gave ear, taking a ten-year-old
and culling him from our world forever.

I'm sorry, Brother. I tried to save you with affidavit, naming
our mother unfit. The sheriff tore you from her arms. Force-fed
a life you couldn't stomach, behind our blind eyes, you gave off
a dark glow to the wrong people and no one knew of your travails.

Cast out by mother, by father, over and over, you inhaled, you imbibed;
you stole and hustled. I saw you nine years later, denim cut-offs, jean
vest, sculpted shoulders, leaning on the Bank of America, one foot
behind on the wall, that thigh bulging. I thought you were dealing.
If only.

I let you move into my garage. Felt in my bones the scrape
of you just the other side of the wall, moving furniture, your stereo,
your Foreigner records, every night 'til sunrise, high on ice. One
night, insomniac with the sounds of you, I knocked and opened
the door, met *un diabolo,* all quivering fury, stepping side to side,
gripping metal baseball bat, angled up over your head, ready to slam
a home run through my skull. I'm still haunted half a life later
by your crazy eyes on me, like a cornered wild thing who will bite
off its own limb to survive.

The Dead and the Living

On the night I met my mother's
third husband, Bob, a carpenter
with scuffed hands and sunburnt
face, his words felt familiar:
I've tried to get your mom off
the booze but she won't listen.
My stepfather who left us—
he'd said that, too.

After the war, after the love,
after giving birth, after raising
a child, at the end of the day,
there's a glass waiting to be
filled, and not a living soul
comes before that.

Song of Orpheus

Trudging up Spruce Street, I stumble
on a manhole cover and I imagine casting
the heavy, bronze plate, pouring orange
ingot into star-studded mold, like a Saint
Christopher's medal, shield and portal
to subterranean sludge. Imagine the young
man who heaves that plate, descending
into the flow of all we don't care to know.
I think of you.

Little brother, you were only ten, waiting
for our mother to come out of that neon
cowboy bar where the hunter groomed
her with beer after beer. Later you said
she'd sold you to him. We didn't see
how Hades took you down to the under
world, how you fell so far you couldn't
get out again.

Thirty years you've scavenged with your
dogs under an overpass at the edge of night.

But you never knew I bargained for your life.
Just fourteen, I entered hell for you, Brother,
breaking the mother-code, singing the terrible
song of truth. I always thought I was the hero
but it was you who bore the malice meted out to
our tribe; it was you who shielded me forever
from the hungry dark.

Tiny Bubbles

It was Vietnam. Pilots would take their R&R in Honolulu, meeting their wives for a weekend of booze, sex, and tears. She went to meet him there, returning with an album by Don Ho, *Tiny Bubbles*, playing it over and over. I was eleven and wanted the song to be about ocean waves. *Make me feel happy, make me feel fine.*

A couple of years after, she was too drunk to help me when I fell and a big screw rammed into the sole of my foot. A doctor put his needle there and drew thread, pulling taut the gut, attending but not healing. An inch-long crescent moonscar of memory no hand could touch. Hobbling on crutches, away from home as much as possible. One Sunday morning, empty bottles and cigarette butts lay strewn across the club carpet—like a movie where John Wayne busts several outlaws in the jaw and destroys the saloon. I sampled whiskey, rum, gin, whatever lay in my path, rolling on the floor, the sad world all giddy and whirling. Now I understood why she drank every day, taking refuge in her tiny bubbles. War doesn't end when your love comes home. Inside her glass, small bubbles rose, quietly drifting toward greater air.

The hole in my foot could never be touched—until my mother died and a Tibetan healer pushed in with her strong thumbs. I told her to beware my tenderfoot but thought, "What if it's all in my head?" Surrendering to her sure hands, I felt I'd cosseted that pain, like an old nail in the wall when you're afraid to pull it out because it might make a bigger hole. I imagined love reaching into my foot, locating the little girl I'd been. "I'll take care of you," I thought. And the pain ceased.

Diapause

A butterfly, orange with scalloped wings, hovers over
white manzanita flowers. *Angled Satyr!* says the naturalist,
waiting by the box elder. A dark fairy flits past. *Black
swallowtail!* I yell. *No, pipevine swallowtail,* says he.
I envy him, imagining this his only care in the world as he
parts green leaves to reveal silver chrysalis cradled in pipevine.
I remember when I was twenty, *I* wanted to be a naturalist.
Instead, I made my bed with Whitman and Yusef, hoving
to cycles of creation and death.

This morning, the Happy Doughnuts lady asked, *Do you pray
to Jesus or to Buddha? You must choose!* She gave me her
picture of Amitapha and urged me to chant. I recalled again
the diapause of those searching days, when certain friends
preached Yogananda, Werner, Suzuki, and Bhagwan.

I'm sorry I didn't know how to be a parent, my father wrote
in his careful hand, *Seek counseling.* His letter left me
cold: I put it in a drawer for thirty years. How does folded
paper, patterned with black-inked words, erase
me? Perhaps he did mean to untie knots but, by then,
I'd already tied up a conception or five, leaving tangled knots
of shame behind, my life's work cut not *out* of me but *for* me:
wrestling with angels.

I never understood what a girl could feel were she the apple
of her father's eye and became an adult before I knew what I'd
missed. Fear was the gift I'd been given and, as if to honor it,
I devoted my life to battle. Like Jacob,
I'd only wanted a blessing!

The Watch Commander

The Watch Commander told us,
It's not a Utopia! at the county jail
orientation. *Don't go in there
and stir up the prisoners! You writers
with your theraputic intentions—
you don't see them after you've
gone back to your cappuccinos,
and these guys are out on the floor,
mothers who abandoned them,
fathers who beat them, all
alive again!*

Yes, that would be me, stirring.
Spreading the embers out.
I'm putting out fires one by one.

Doesn't he realize I also go
back out there, on the floor
of my life, singed by memories
of beloved hands striking,
of being asked to choose
between belt and spatula?

Meantime, my life's love, once
a rakish, punkish writer of songs,
sources tea to soothe the souls
of his customers. He tells me
he's fragile and I respect that.
Keeping calm is important to him.

I want to know how the vertebrae
in my neck might feel had I not
been struck. I want to feel the space
between connective tissue, let
the gap between spirit and self
be *lived*. Drown in the water I'm pouring
on the coals of a good enough life.
I'm still a prisoner, albeit a lucky one.

Death Portrait

Awakening: How did a father wake on the day after the mother of his children said, *Don't come home?* Did he lie in his metal bunk under wool navy blanket, his body stiff, reaching for pictures of his daughter and son, each bombing mission risked for them? How did a mother wake on the first morning after her children were taken away? Did she push the covers off, hand groping for her watch, measure coffee from the can, light a Pall Mall, drawing smoke in, like punishment? How did a brother, virginal young boy, wake in the dawn, next to a man who'd used him and promised love? Cold comfort and no one can know. A smattering of dust brings angels of snow.

God's Wounds: The *curandero* held my head, placed warm fingers in my ears, a candle flickered shadows across my eyelids. One question flowed from a place before personality: why the savage world? Perhaps God bears a wound and we must choose: flee into despair, hurting others forever, or keep vigil with fire 'til the fever subsides and the embers of stars sing in our being, sighing each note in the music of us all.

Death Portrait: Love carries a picture of death in her breast pocket. It's not morbid to do this; it's a matter of life. In meditation, little bits of oxygen work their way through—and the body, as though answering a call, lets the stomach gurgle a song, and the spaces in the sinus begin to tick and pop. When time permits, love senses her source.

Youth with White Deck Shoes

Please don't pick the skin off your face
as you pace in the doorway of the Chinese
restaurant, words spilling fast onto concrete,
your mouth in motion—so affected I can't
understand a thing. Is it that you're hawking
your wares and I don't get the peculiar-to-your-
trade cry? So unlike the roasted corn-on-a-stick
seller in Mexico—*Heloteeeee!*—who stalks
the cobbled, dusty streets, buckets at the ends
of husky arms, hollering his wide-mouth song,
pure tone from barrel chest, his prayer at dusk—
calienteeeee, dulceeee, andaleeeee!

Hot, sweet, good.
You want to be all those things in your white
deck shoes, but someone hurt you,
so you can't.

Where the Power Lies

*Please call the county coroner, he wrote. Kirk hasn't picked
up his mail—he could be dead, for all we know.* Once more,
I'm the good daughter searching for her father's son.

After pushing a few buttons on my computer, I locate him:
SF Chronicle picture of transient jungle at Gilman overpass,
leaning on a bike, hair straggly, still alive.

> Meantime, a boy I used to know—grade school classmate
> of my daughter's—sits in an Oakland courtroom today
> as his parents plead, *Your Honor, we didn't do right*
>
> *by our boy, Sir.* They search for the right words
> to show they understand where the power lies to save
> the life of their child. They need to believe this.

*Please don't send me any more poems about him.
It might help you but it hurts me.* If only there were
a Judge sitting on his bench, coffee at his left hand,

gavel in his right, who had the say to give my father
back his child and me my brother. What is the procedure
to recover one misplaced life?

Attitude

During the interview, I ask him about his favorite maneuver.
*Well, I have to say it was dive bombing: I had to locate the red flare
dropped by Recon—it was just a dot, really—and point the nose
at the target, dropping at a 60-degree angle from 20,000 to 3,000 feet,
deliver the payload, and pull up sharp.*

I calm my breath, imagine gravity, ask my father: "Did you ever get
vertigo?" *No, but one time I did become disoriented.
My bombardier navigator… See, in the dark, the red dot was so tiny…
and the instrument panel was red, too.*

He stares at wrinkled hands, compressing lips that smacked
buss kisses in the scratchy chair of back then. I remember
how he slammed our skulls together—mine and my brother's.
How he threw him out at thirteen, again at fourteen. Sweat
trickles down my sides, as it always does when we talk.
I've always resented you, he said once, as though I might
take comfort in that cipher forever encoded on my guts.

Attitude: truculent behavior; a resentful or antagonistic manner.

*I don't know what happened. My bombardier—well,
he was completely silent as the plane climbed straight up.
In another second, we were going to stall. See, the plane
can't maintain lift in vertical…I lost focus.
Then, my bombardier…my best friend, really, said one word:
"attitude." That's what saved us. Attitude.*

Attitude: orientation of the aircraft relative to the earth's horizon.

What was the best quality of your father?
He never abandoned his post.
And your mother? *I can't think of one.* He tells me how,
as a boy, he put his body between his mother and his father's
blows. *She wouldn't forgive him for something, wouldn't let*

him forget it. She'd scold and he'd explode. Because of her, my dad had to be someone he didn't want to be.

Attitude: position of the body implying an action or mental state.

Yes, he did his duty, paid for college, loved me, but he inhabited a grudge I never understood. Because of me, my dad had to be someone *he* didn't want to be. I face him, seeking answers on wars we inherited and the ways we each had to fight.

Green Heron, Hunting

A ringing in my ears, an aperture allowing too much
light has ruined my focus and frazzled boundaries
between me and the world and for the first time
in my life, I want to die. I dip into sleep, dream
a monster outside my cage changes into a brownish-green
bird I've never seen. Upon waking, I see the same bird
at Jewel Lake, drawing the net of its gaze across crayfish
under glazed surface, preparing to strike from the rushes.
Green Heron, says a bird watcher, *the ugliest bird ever.*
Unruffled, placing stick toes with precision, the heron
lifts each foot, sunlight refracting through emerald eye.
Humans wander off, voices humming like gnats; at last,
silence. Let the demon become a friend, let the green heron
teach me to hunt the quarry of my lost quiet
and all the sustenance it can give.

Coming to My Senses

        What if I did use my husband and children as band-aids
to cover a gaping wound? Isn't that love? When I was
four, I hurled five kittens into a dry swimming pool.
One by one, I swung them by the tail and released.
Their little mews and closing eyes, I understood.

Your eyes see detail with the clarity and precision of an eighteen-year said the Know-Your-Age-by-Color Discernment Quiz.
That night I dreamt white lilies, brown chocolate, azure river
as I was shown a word I'd never heard, *achoya*.
From early Sanskrit, it means obedience.

        It was *Yes, Ma'am and No, Sir.* No backtalk.
And though I found rapture in their music,
Beethoven looked so mad, to listen was to fall
in love and fear punishment at once.

        I forgive them for hitting and throwing. Honor
them; they had their reasons. Just as I had reason
to force five new lives from this world.
Lives I can't tell even you about.

But I always knew my soul saw 64 Crayola colors—
periwinkle blue at first light, sky blue at noon, salmon
at sundown, brick red at dusk, as I flew with midnight
blue swifts, sky-clotting en route to Mexico, over sea green
gulf with whitest sand dappled with violet and magenta
shells, whorled and circling in my burnt sienna heart.

Ghost Breast

Ghost breast of luxuriant
youth, you are not.
Negative space, no.
Spare part, salvage
of diagnosis past, they
put you in a freezer, encoded
with name and number.

I know we parted ways but
did I thank you for all you gave?
First food for my children,
you gave them myself,
translated, substantiated.
You kept your twin company,
endowed that human love of symmetry
to my then perfect body,
bedecked a changing girlhood,
held up under braless halter tops,
and, though you never meant to, saluted
many an admiring eye.

Sincerest gratitude is due to you
for blazing the trail of rapture
and its ensuing bonds,
claiming nothing for yourself,
ever generous, tome
of two together,
now one alone. And, yes,
I still feel you.

Moon on the North Platte

He sleeps, mouth open, hand on my leg,
and the earth—valleys, pinnacles, plateaus,

lakes, rivers, roads—lies dark thirty
thousand feet below our window.

I love your little breast, he'd said, after.
Maybe one day you'll let me see.

But, he can't know the scar, the drawing down
my chest, dry plain of once-full riparian stream.

I never knew you felt that way! But, it's a kind
of war; you wouldn't shame a soldier for replacing a limb.

Looking out my smudged portal, a spark silvers
the night, a headlight perhaps. No. Hint of mercury,

undulating, sketching on black river. I'm that girl
again, sitting crosslegged on the carpet, enchanted

by Captain Kangaroo's magic drawing board.
The North Platte drains the Front Range, tumbling

down from snowy crags, moon in pursuit, gilding
the river, coaxing shimmer as only reflected sunlight

can. Tomorrow, maybe I'll answer the surgeon's
voicemail at last. Fill the dam one more time.

What's Lost

And where is my hummingbird nest?
Lichens stud the tiny pouch, bits of dust,
pillow fuzz for babies. The Mazda key
is missing again and I'm turning pants inside out.
My kids roll their eyes and begin counting.

We moved from town to town, red brick
houses, yellow Mayflower vans, marble-top
dresser wrapped in blue quilts, grandmother's
fairy books, Aunt Min's needlepoint, and my
records: *Meet the Beatles, Dave Clark Five.*
My chore: checking numbers on stickers
as movers carried out Navy orders.
Florida, Mississippi, South Carolina, Texas,
Virginia, California, Missouri, Kansas.
Will you all welcome our new student?
Nineteen schools: a child's tour of duty
across a nation at war.

When I was 25, my grandmother sent a list
of all the places I'd claimed since coming of age,
her careful handwriting filled the folded page.
Love-lost streets, numbers of mistaken pregnancies,
cities of abandoned paths, coded
by loss of brother and breast.

When I lose something, how can I explain
to my children, who grew up in one house
in this leafy college town, played Ghost
in the Graveyard with freckled friends, filled
the basement with Legos and plastic lions,
basked in unsplintered light of parents' marriage,
wars fought in far lands by volunteer forces,

it's my Iron Butterfly, my white chenille bedspread
with phoenix at the center, piano and dance lessons
postponed, the grand piano sold,
the child looking for a nest,
however fragile.

Riding Waves

The waves gather up surf scoters, black ducks with yellow
bills, floating in quaint quadrille, rising, falling, unperturbed,
each roller a charger cantering to shore, neck arched, *destrier*
mane of spray flying, only to founder on land in roil of foam

or throw a shoe on jagged rocks, rocks that splintered ships, sailors
wracked to starfish and barnacle, earth's sharp bones. Down
the strand, three figures step into the swell, paddling for a smooth
channel. One turns his board, parts the water with small hands, races

to leap astride, only to fall back, the riderless courser surging on.
The next surfer meets towering wave, jumps to his feet, riding
the glittering berm, only to be thrown under, board spinning in mist,
sinking into white churn. The last one sits, bareback, legs dangling

over her mount, waits for her break, perhaps content to simply keep
company with bobbing birds, lacking urge to conquer. All history lies
on that advancing line, implacable wave of everything, white Percheron
of meaning, while humans dare to drown or, like the surf scoter, call

it nothing. Still, there is one thing: how the riders huddle together
on the sea's vast flank as they consider angle and tack, three small
specks—a family—hovering over the unknown, bound not only
by fear and drive, but also a certain mighty happiness.

Yearly Rituals

Every year on this day, he claims me.
Every year, I take my heart's temperature,

say a prayer to the god who didn't take care
of my little brother, wherever he may be,

say *Happy Birthday* to the small boy I loved
when we were given into each other's keeping.

Twelve months of days, twelve months
of ways I can justify the parting of kin.

Nature or nurture, onions in a mesh bag,
layers underneath papery duff, rubbing

against each other in a net of blame.
Can't explain, as Billie sang, and one

day soon, there'll be no one who
remembers or cares to understand.

Tape

I

When the hurricanes came, my mother would tape
the windows, criss-cross with big Xs and fill
the bathtub full of water. We'd pack the white VW
and head for the Travelodge with the sleepy bear
overlooking the parking lot. I was ten and eating
blueberry pancakes at the diner was fun until one
time we came back to Pensacola Beach and found
the concrete block house three doors down gone.
*It exploded from pressure when the tornadoes
hit,* said my mother. *They forgot to leave a window
open.* I made a note: huge storms carry smaller calamities
around with them. And it was true about Vietnam.

II

Every A-6 ordinance aimed, my father dropping in a nose
dive and every napalm bomb released, my stepfather
cruising in his F-4, exploded at home as my mother,
like Ruby in *Don't Take Your Love to Town*, rolled
black fishnets over her thighs and drove away over the
speed bumps in our blue station wagon.

Waging her own war on me, my blonde mother Scotch
taped my brown hair in a curl against my cheek at night.
At the beach, she said, You look like a tank and grabbed
the flesh of my leg to show me. As Christmas tears
fell into her rum and coke, I opened my presents slowly,
savoring the tiny happiness. My little brother cried because
he'd opened all his. My mother glared with her blank blue
stare, said *Kathy doesn't deserve Christmas presents.* I ran to my
room and wouldn't come out.

A regular ritual: sitting on her flowered bedspread, listening
to cassette tapes sent from strange addresses—
NAVACTS, NY, NY—recorded on bombing missions by
our broken stepdad. The recorder spindles turned on the bed
as she begged me to sing *Noche de Paz*, in *Espanol*
and, against my loud protests, tell *him* I'd had my first period.
When the war ended, everything would go back to how it used to be.

III

I left her
at fourteen and sojourned fifteen years, seeking
the quarry of my heart: stealing Slicker lipstick, playing
Joni, steel strings digging grooves into my fingertips, flaring
femme fatale, just like my mother, and hating her for it.
I arched my back through lover after lover, pyroclastic
blasts that left no trace.

On metamorphic rock, erupted by volcanic explosions,
I discovered hidden petroglyphs and studied one for years:
the hunter on the wall. A stick figure aiming his tiny
arrow at a mastodon about to mow him down—
was I the hunter or the target?

IV

I justified loose margins with Transcendentalism, Buddhism, and jazz,
spinning *A Love Supreme*—a scholarly nature girl, onyx nose ring,
tripping to *Waltz of the Flowers* at the San Diego Zoo, frolicking
in white-gold Pacific waves. Once, at a Rajneesh meditation,
my docile saxophone lover and I jumped blindfolded for an hour
to a tape of drums to ignite primal feelings until I heard his voice
scream *Fuck you, Bitch!!* I kept hearing the old Tex Ritter song,
I hate you one and all, ooh, blast your eyes!

Words fell from my ordered page; I went two-stepping
to *bandas nortenas* in East Oakland with my *novio mojado*,
a boxer with a scar from a gunshot wound, who taught me to fight.
You are for everybody, mi Reina! I fled him and took up *charanga*
with a Venezuelan charmer; he taped my mouth closed, opening
me only when needed. Thanks to him, I began to punch
my father out when I danced alone.

In time, I located the blue eye of the hurricane,
suffered the three marriages: self, true companion, vocation.
When the lab report came, I let the hunters cut me
and bind my chest with tape.
It blew over,
like a cyclone might,
if you leave a window open.

Vanishing Point

In Mexico at night, there are sounds.
Alone in this room, this
town, this country, where
no one knows my name,
seeking the girl I once knew,
I hear clanking pipes hammering
in the walls, dogs bellowing,
church bells rung by hand,
vibrating with human secrets, cherry
bombs to honor *La Virgen,* laughter
and then some.
But, none of it is loud.
What I hear most is the sounding
of my thoughts, humming
like power lines along a
two-lane highway, traveling
at the speed of light, to gather all
the memories in, strands woven
into tough cords that stretch
from pole to pole.

I see her lying down
in the back seat of the old
family Buick, looking out,
mesmerized
by the rhythmic bobbing
of the lines, and the way the poles,
those captured moments, pop
into view and vanish,
crowded out by the next
and the next until I know
the vanishing point is just over the
horizon—where I hope
to rearrange them into
circles, Venn Diagrams
of overlapping
love.

Kathryn Jordan is a writer, musician, and teacher from Berkeley, CA. She got her MA from UC Berkeley, then took a break from writing to raise a family and teach English, American roots and choral music and guitar for many years. She created a curriculum for middle school that integrated singing, music theory, history and writing to share with youth the story of African-American music and its impact on American life. Vocationally promiscuous, Kathryn performs in coffee houses, musical theatre, and is currently studying improv. When a poem requires it, Kathryn has been known to burst into song. She is an avid birder, backpacker and photographer. She has studied with Robert Hass, Dorianne Laux, Joe Millar, Marie Howe and continues to work with Alison Luterman and Ellen Bass.

www.ingramcontent.com/pod-product-compliance
Lightning Source LLC
LaVergne TN
LVHW041513070426
835507LV00012B/1537